I Am Albert Einstein

By Grace Norwich

Illustrated by
Ute Simon

SCHOLASTIC INC.

If you purchased this book without a cover, you should be aware that this book is stolen property. It was reported as "unsold and destroyed" to the publisher, and neither the author nor the publisher has received any payment for this "stripped book."

No part of this publication may be reproduced, stored in a retrieval system, or transmitted in any form or by any means, electronic, mechanical, photocopying, recording, or otherwise, without written permission of the publisher. For information regarding permission, write to Scholastic Inc., Attention: Permissions Department, 557 Broadway, New York, NY 10012.

Copyright © 2012 by Scholastic Inc.

All rights reserved. Published by Scholastic Inc. SCHOLASTIC and associated logos are trademarks and/or registered trademarks of Scholastic Inc.

ISBN 978-0-545-40575-1

10 9 8 7 6 5 4   13 14 15 16 17/0

Printed in the U.S.A.   40
First printing, August 2012

Cover illustration by Mark Fredrickson
Interior illustrations by Ute Simon
Book design by Kay Petronio

Contents

Introduction 4
People You Will Meet 8
Time Line 10
Chapter One: Not Your Average Kid 12
Chapter Two: The Trouble with Being
    a Genius 30
Chapter Three: It's a Miracle! 46
Chapter Four: Space Bender 62
Chapter Five: Putting All the Pieces
    Together 76
Map of Europe 1936 94
10 Things You Should Know About
    Einstein 96
10 MORE Things That Are Pretty Cool to Know . 100
Places to Visit 104
Bibliography 106
Glossary 108
Index 110

Introduction

When I was twenty-six years old, I changed our ideas about the universe. People later called it my miracle year because, while working as a clerk in a government patent office, I came up with new equations and formulas that would eventually lead to all sorts of inventions, from cell phones to space travel. They included the theory of relativity and my famous equation $E = mc^2$.

So you can say I was a success, perhaps even the most famous scientist of all time. As proof my name has become another word for "genius." But I didn't start out that way. In fact when I was a little boy my teachers didn't think I would amount to very much.

That's because I wasn't like everyone else. Okay, I was strange. I didn't enjoy playing games with the other students and thought

class was a total bore (which my teachers did not appreciate). Instead I preferred to spend time alone—thinking.

Sure, I loved my little sister, Maja, and my parents. But I found a big and exciting world right inside my own head. Although my area of science was physics—the study of matter and energy, including how objects behave in motion—my mind was my best laboratory. (I was actually such a klutz in real labs that I once caused an explosion.) That's because I always had a huge imagination. I pictured the most amazing things, such as what it would be like to travel on a beam of light, and asked big questions, like how the universe worked.

Then I spent years patiently looking at patterns and working on complicated math problems to find the answers. It wasn't easy. I was wrong many times before I was right. But I was never afraid to make mistakes. You'll always make mistakes when you try something new. It's just part of the process.

Fueled by my legendary curiosity, my discoveries in science led to lots of practical inventions, such as smoke alarms and automatic doors. They also led to faraway places, like the origin of the universe and expanding galaxies. And it all started in my mind. "Imagination is more important than knowledge," I once said. "Knowledge is limited. Imagination encircles the world." I am Albert Einstein.

People You Will Meet

ALBERT EINSTEIN:
The most famous physicist in history, who used his mind to make amazing new discoveries that changed science and the world forever.

PAULINE EINSTEIN:
Albert's mother, who gave her son a love of music by making him stick with violin lessons. Playing the violin became one of his life's passions.

HERMANN EINSTEIN:
Albert's father, who ran a gas and electrical supply company in Munich with his brother Jakob. He gave a compass to young Albert as a gift, the mechanics of which sparked a lifelong curiosity and passion for problem solving.

JAKOB EINSTEIN*: Albert's uncle, an engineer and inventor. He had a scientific mind and would often make up complex math problems for his little nephew to solve.

MAJA EINSTEIN: Albert's sister, with whom he had a close relationship. She never seemed to mind being in the shadow of her famous big brother.

MAX TALMUD: A poor medical student who had meals at the Einstein home. He introduced young Albert to geometry and to the writings of famous philosophers.

MILEVA MARIC: Albert's first wife and the only female student in the physics department of their college. She and her husband had a lot of common interests, though this wasn't enough to keep their marriage together. After she gave birth to two sons—Hans Albert and Eduard—she and Albert divorced.

MARCEL GROSSMANN: An organized math student at Albert's college, who became Albert's friend for life. He helped Albert reach his goals by sharing his class notes and finding a job for the hapless genius.

ELSA LÖWENTHAL: Albert's first cousin and second wife. Her cheerful disposition and ability to overlook Albert's flaws made her a good partner.

* Artist's rendering

Time Line

March 14, 1879
Albert Einstein is born in Ulm, Germany.

1880
The Einstein family moves to Munich, Germany.

1881
Albert's sister, Maja, is born.

1896
He enrolls in college at the Swiss Federal Polytechnic Institute in Zurich, where he still has a bad attitude about school.

1900
Albert graduates from college but struggles to find a job.

1902
With the help of college pal Marcel Grossmann's father, Albert lands a job at the Swiss patent office.

1914
Albert moves to Berlin, and World War I breaks out.

1919
February 14, 1919
He and Mileva are divorced.

May 29, 1919
A solar eclipse proves Albert's general theory of relativity correct and makes him a science superstar.

June 2, 1919
Albert and Elsa Löwenthal are married.

1921
Albert wins the Nobel Prize in physics for his discovery of the photoelectric effect.

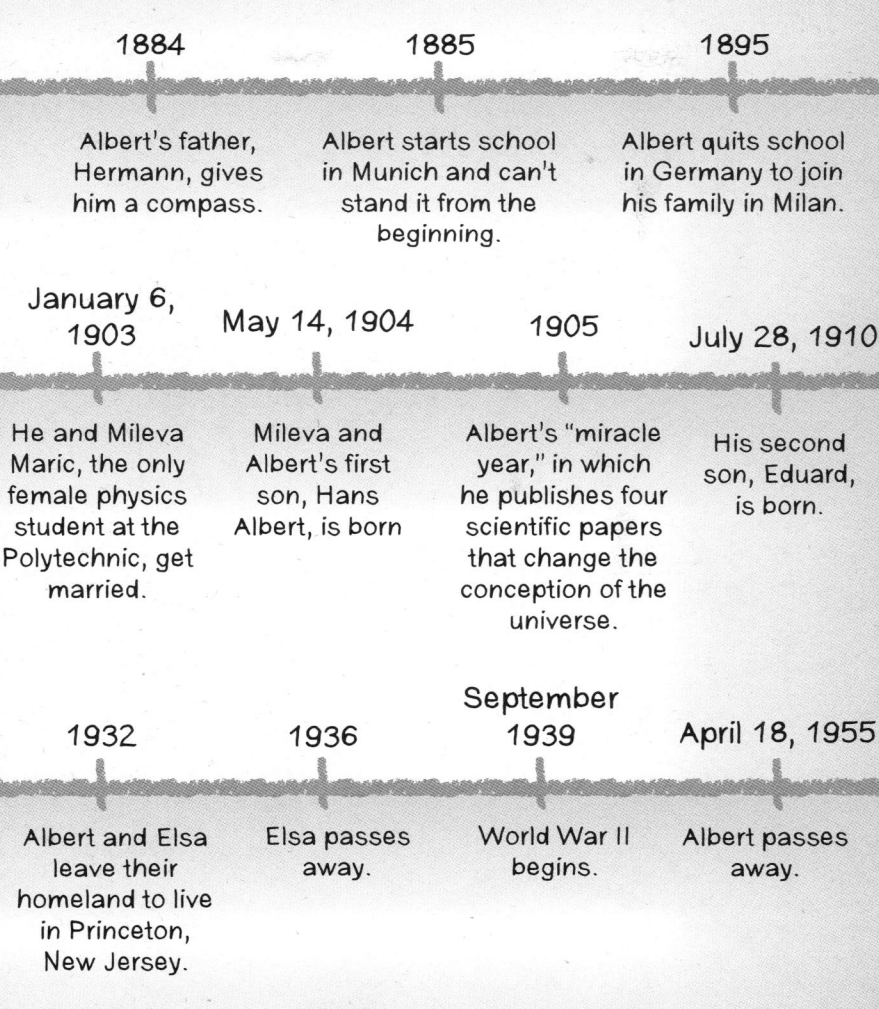

CHAPTER ONE

Not Your Average Kid

Albert Einstein's brain might not have been bigger than anyone else's, but his head sure was. Born on March 14, 1879, in the small German town of Ulm, the baby genius's head seemed too big for his body. His parents, Hermann and Pauline, worried that their son might be unusual. Albert certainly turned out to be different—but not in a way his parents ever imagined.

When Albert turned one, the Einsteins

moved to the larger city of Munich, where Albert continued to worry his parents. He didn't babble or say little words like other babies. Hermann and Pauline took him to see many doctors, but no one could find anything wrong with him. Albert apparently didn't speak a word until the birth of his sister, Maja. The story goes that his parents told him they were bringing home a "new toy." When he first saw his sister, the previously silent Albert blurted out, "Where are the wheels?"

Even after Albert began to speak, his way of talking was strange. He would whisper sentences a few times to himself, as if he were rehearsing what he wanted to say, before he would speak out loud. His slow way of speaking made people think he wasn't smart.

Albert wasn't too concerned about the way he talked. An extremely shy and quiet child, he preferred to play by himself anyway. The housekeeper gave him the nickname Father Bore because he hardly made a peep all day.

When he did express himself as a small child, it was often with anger. Albert, who grew up to be one of the most peace-loving men of all time, had a very bad temper as a kid. He was especially prone to throwing things at Maja. Eventually, the siblings became best friends.

Albert's family loved him, quirks and all. Hermann, a businessman, owned a gas and electrical supply company with his brother Jakob, who was an engineer and inventor. It was a great partnership since Hermann could handle the commercial side of the business while Jakob worked on **patents** for electric meters, new lamps, circuit breakers, and other things. Pauline, who grew up in a wealthy family, brought culture to the Einstein clan.

She played piano very well. Hoping to pass her love of music on to her son, she gave him a violin when he was about six. Albert fought his mandatory lessons at first—he didn't like people telling him what to do. Soon enough, the violin became a major source of joy (especially when he played duets with his mother on the piano, or any pieces by his favorite composer, Mozart). The violin was a lifelong pleasure for

FLASH OF GENIUS

Albert was born in the same year Thomas Edison introduced the first electric light!

Albert and something he did at all hours of the day and night to clear his mind when trying to work out a difficult problem.

The gift his father gave him when he was five years old was much more of an immediate hit. Albert, who had been sick, was recovering in bed. So his dad wanted to get him something to cheer him up. He pulled a shiny new compass out of his pocket. Albert stared at the little mechanism with a needle that always pointed north no matter how he turned it. *Why?* He was desperate to know how it worked. Hermann explained that Earth is like a big magnet with a force all around us that we can't see or feel but which pulls the pointer north. The answer didn't satisfy Albert at all. The idea of a hidden force set Albert's mind going around as fast as the pointer on the compass. Where did the magnetism come from, and how did it get into their house? Little did his father know that the compass was the start of an amazing quest to discover the hidden secrets of the universe.

Albert's curiosity about the compass came as no surprise to Hermann. In fact, he encouraged it. So did Pauline. The Einstein family had

a deep love of learning and respect for the intellect. The first step to gaining knowledge was asking questions.

Albert's kind of critical thinking was *not* appreciated at the school he attended when he turned six years old. Albert had never been an obedient student. He once threw a chair at his tutor, who promptly quit and left the house. His new elementary school wasn't any more promising. His parents chose it because it was close enough for Albert to walk to. But as the only Jewish kid in a class of seventy students at the Catholic school, he was an immediate outsider.

The other boys teased him, sometimes surprising him on his way home from school to attack and insult him. Prejudice against Jews, which is called anti-Semitism, was on the rise in Germany. Albert couldn't believe that his classmates thought all Jewish people were

born with the same traits. Albert had a lot of Jewish people in his family and each of them was different from the next. He preferred to be by himself anyway, he reasoned.

Things weren't much better for Albert inside the classroom. At that time, school in Germany was very, very strict. Students had to stand and wait for their teacher to arrive and settle into his own seat before they could sit down. If a

student fell asleep (although it was practically impossible on those hard wooden benches), he received a painful smack against the wrists or shins with a wooden cane. Other offenses that merited the same punishment were giving the wrong answer one too many times, talking out of turn, making a wisecrack, or whispering to a friend.

Beyond the teasing and the cane, the worst part of school for Albert was the actual learning. Back then, school was all about memorizing facts and repeating them. It was so bad that Albert called his teachers sergeants because of the way they drilled the kids in class. He found the drills boring and wanted to ask questions to learn the material for himself. At home he was encouraged to ask questions by his parents, so you can imagine how confused Albert was when his teachers found him rude because he asked too many of them in class. He always got very good grades (he was a genius after all!), but his teachers found him infuriating.

Albert was smart enough— or perhaps lucky enough— to find wonderful teachers outside the classroom. He found a kindred spirit in his uncle Jakob, who invented

complicated math problems that Albert would spend days working on alone in his room until he solved them. Jakob was amazed by how quickly his nephew grasped new and difficult mathematical concepts (in fact it wouldn't be long before Albert surpassed his uncle's math abilities). He realized that Albert not only could do the problems he gave him, but also *loved* to do them. Understanding that Albert thirsted for knowledge, Jakob introduced him to the world of electricity and magnetism that was the family business. Light and how it traveled became an obsession for his nephew almost instantly.

Another huge influence in Albert's young life was Max Talmud, who regularly visited the Einsteins to enjoy home-cooked meals. It was a traditional European Jewish custom to

invite a poor student over to eat. Typically it would have been a religious student, but since the Einsteins weren't a religious family they kept up the tradition by hosting Max, who was a medical student. Max took an interest in little Albert and gave him a book on **geometry**, which Albert worked through in no time. Max

followed that book with one on higher math, or **algebra** as it's often called. Albert tore through that as well.

Albert, who adored his time alone, was a huge reader—a fact that Max seized upon by giving him many kinds of books and not just ones on math. Albert loved the way a book opened up new worlds, far beyond school and

even home. He read about **geology**, **chemistry**, and **physics**. When he was just thirteen years old, Max gave him the *Critique of Pure Reason* by the German philosopher Immanuel Kant, which is every bit as hard as it sounds from the title. Albert consumed the book like it was a novel, and it affected the way he thought about human beings for the rest of his life.

While the boys at school called him names and his teachers berated him, Albert was far away in his mind. Who cares about teasing when you are considering the philosophical question of whether man really has free will, or imagining what it would be like to travel on a beam of light?

CHAPTER TWO

The Trouble with Being a Genius

Despite the growing use of electric light, the Einstein brothers' business was not going well. Hermann worked hard, but he wasn't the best businessman. They needed to find another place with more opportunity to make money. When Albert turned fifteen, Hermann decided the place was Milan. Moving to Italy must have been an exciting prospect for Albert. The sunny city was filled with good food and modern technology. There was only one problem: Albert wasn't moving with the rest of his family.

He had to stay behind in Munich, a place he didn't much care for, to finish high school, a place he really, really didn't care for. The decision was made, however, and that was that. Hermann and Pauline wanted their son to get his diploma.

If Albert thought school was bad before, after his family left Germany it only got worse. He was lonely and miserable. In class, Albert asked even more questions and talked out of turn all the time.

Albert, always strong-headed and sure of himself, took matters into his own hands and quit school (some sources say he was expelled) after one term away from his family. His teachers didn't protest. In fact, they were happy to see the troublemaker go. His parents, whom he surprised in Italy, were *not* happy. Without

a high-school degree, they worried he wouldn't amount to much more than a daydreamer.

While Albert was content to simply spend time with his family in Italy, Hermann wanted his son to be a little more productive. Since Albert wasn't attending school, his father encouraged him to learn about the family business. He could work with his uncle on

his inventions or do sums for his father's bookkeeping. Albert did help out for a while, but his heart wasn't in it. Throughout his life, he was never interested in the practical side of work. He was inspired by ideas and how far he could take them.

Perhaps the experience of working with his father and uncle motivated him to return to school, but he found a Swiss school that was the opposite of his drill-focused German school. Albert lived with a family in Aarau, Switzerland, and finished high school much to his parents' relief.

Albert loved Switzerland and decided to enroll in the physics program at the Swiss Federal Polytechnic Institute in Zurich. The future science superstar continued to be a troublemaker, annoying teachers, cutting classes, and setting off an explosion in the lab after ignoring important rules. He was even

flunked by a physics professor for attitude issues!

In class, he might have been a rude know-it-all. But back in his room, he was in awe of the work of the greatest physicists of his time. He read everything he could on the latest discoveries in his particular branch of science. He felt like his classes weren't taking into account all the new things physicists were learning about—particularly light.

Skipping class at the Polytechnic gave Albert plenty of time to become more social and make friends, many of whom became his lifelong pals. He thoroughly enjoyed sitting in cafés, drinking coffee and debating scientific theories with his classmates. One of his best friends, Marcel Grossmann, did more than just entertain Albert. A year older than Albert and an extremely organized math student, Marcel gave his friend notes from all the classes he

A Brief History of Physics

- **THE GREEKS:** The first Western attempts to provide a rational, nonreligious explanation for how nature worked (like the sun, moon, and stars) came with the Greeks in 600 BC.

- **THE RENAISSANCE:** Galileo Galilei (1564–1642) is considered to have started modern science by changing the role of scientists from explaining *why* something happens to describing *what* is happening.  His other big change was to use mathematics as the description for natural phenomena, and experiments to see if the description is correct.

- **BEGINNING OF CLASSICAL PHYSICS:** Isaac Newton, born in 1642 (the year Galileo died), discovered basic laws of nature that are true throughout the entire universe. They are the **three laws of motion** and the **universal law of gravity**, which states that the bigger the objects and the closer they are to each other, the stronger the attraction between them.

- **ELECTROMAGNETISM:** In 1752 Benjamin Franklin used a kite to collect the charge from a thundercloud and store it in a jar! In addition to showing a connection between electricity and magnetism, he figured out that electrical charge comes in two types, negative and positive, with like charges repelling each other and opposites attracting. This opened up the world of electricity to future scientists.

had missed. If Marcel hadn't been so generous, Albert would almost certainly have flunked out.

While Albert was busy making friends, he also fell in love. Mileva Maric, the only woman in his class, had been a child **prodigy** in math. She was a unique person for her time since not many women went to college and even fewer studied science or math. The couple spent long hours talking about math and science as

they hiked in the nearby Alps. Albert's curly hair was always messy and his clothes were wrinkled or poorly fitted. Meanwhile, Mileva had a limp and often got sick. But neither of them cared.

Some men at that time would not have wanted to be with a female scientist. On the contrary, Albert not only supported Mileva's education, he loved studying with her.

Unfortunately, when it came time to graduate, Mileva failed her exams. (Albert came in fourth in a class of five students.) It didn't matter to Albert, who was head over heels in love.

He wanted to marry Mileva, but when he graduated from college in 1900, he couldn't find a job. Without employment, there was no way he could support a wife and family. Albert's goal when he finished school had always been

to become a professor, but he hadn't exactly been a model student. His teachers refused to recommend him for any teaching position. They thought he was a smart aleck, not a genius.

The next period of his life was difficult, as Albert struggled to find a way to make money. Not only did he fail at every career attempt, including tutoring—even when he offered the first lesson for free!—but his parents also disapproved of him marrying Mileva because she was three years older than him and sickly. On top of all that, his father's business went bankrupt. Albert had no idea what he was going to do. His mind was filled with limitless possibilities, but his future felt hopeless.

CHAPTER THREE

It's a Miracle!

If Albert didn't already know Marcel was a true friend, there was no doubt after Marcel helped him land a job. Albert's break came through Marcel Grossmann's father, who was friendly with the director of the Swiss patent office. A patent is a government-issued document that allows an inventor to make and sell an invention, and prevents others from copying it. Albert was hired by the director in 1902 to make sure that ideas people sent in for new inventions actually worked. (He became a citizen of Switzerland that same year.)

Thrilled, Albert promised in a letter to Marcel to "do everything in my power not to disgrace your recommendation." No more bad-attitude Albert. The time he spent looking for work seemed to have given him a sense of appreciation.

Patent clerk was a perfect job for him—not because he loved going over other people's inventions. He did like looking for the flaws in someone's argument, and a lot of the subjects people were working on (such as electricity and energy) excited him. The best feature of his position, however, was the fact that it allowed him time to work on his own science projects. Because Albert was able to get his patent work done in roughly three hours, he had the rest of the day to spend on his experiments.

Albert didn't need a lab to do his research since it all took place in his head. He liked to

call them thought experiments. He would come up with problems, imagine solutions, and then do the complex math to see if he was right. He did need lots and lots of paper for his math problems, but whenever anyone walked by his desk, he'd quickly shove the papers aside and pretend he was doing patent work.

With a steady paycheck, Albert was finally able to marry Mileva in 1903, and just a year later they welcomed their first son, Hans

Albert. Although Albert wanted Mileva to continue as a scientist, she failed her exam for a second time and so instead focused her efforts on taking care of Albert and their new child.

Meanwhile, Albert was concentrating all his efforts on making the biggest scientific breakthrough of the twentieth century. He continued to be fascinated with light and the new study of particles in electromagnetic theory.

The problem that was bothering scientists had to do with electromagnetic theory—equations that describe how electricity, light, and magnetism work. Experiments proved that light always traveled at the same speed. But this contradicted Newton's laws of motion, the basis of all physics, which stated that speed changes under different circumstances. Scientists found over and over again that the speed of light doesn't change. Still, Newton couldn't be wrong. What was the answer?

Albert happened upon it in his streetcar. There was a big clock tower he always looked at during the ride, but one day it got him thinking. If he traveled away from the clock at the speed of light, light from the clock face would never catch up with him and so the hands would appear frozen in time. However, if he traveled at the speed of light while wearing a watch, the timepiece on his wrist would be moving with him at the same speed and would appear to tell time normally.

This was the beginning of Albert's really big idea: the principle of relativity.

Relativity means "comparing one situation or object to another." In Albert's case, how things appear is relative to the person looking. It was the birth of a brand-new concept of how space and time work together.

What The?

If you read about the special theory of relativity and all the words made sense, but you still don't understand it, you aren't alone. Most scientists couldn't understand it at the time and most people still can't. That's because many of Albert's theories were counterintuitive, meaning they are opposite of what makes sense to us. When physicists do mathematical computations and observe physical phenomena, they work. However, they are hard for us to imagine.

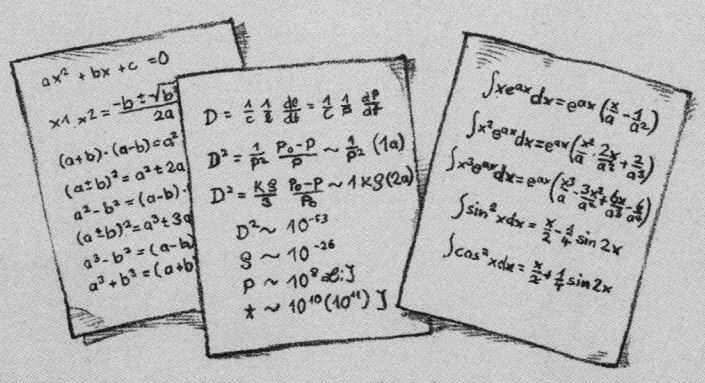

After the idea struck, Albert set to work furiously and in only five weeks had written his paper on the special theory of relativity. In it he argued that if the speed of light doesn't change and Newton's laws of physics don't change, then the element that *does* change is time. So if you are traveling at the speed of light, time stands still. Space and time are connected as one, space-time.

So what was the response from the physics community to Albert's special theory of

relativity and his other three papers in 1905? Scientists basically ignored his work, which was difficult to imagine and went against common knowledge.

Critics, or lack of them, had never stopped Albert before, and they didn't stop him then. The following year, he published six more papers, and in 1907, ten! Still, no school wanted to hire the patent clerk (not even as a high-school math teacher).

Slowly, Albert's ideas began to take hold

as other scientists set about proving them on a small scale in labs or using them to further other theories (those were the goals he always had for them). Finally, in 1909, he was offered the job he'd been hoping for ever since he left school—an academic position. The University of Zurich gave him a newly created position, professor in theoretical physics.

The university's newest junior professor wasn't the most organized teacher. Often his lectures were little more than scraps of paper in his pocket. What he lacked in order, he made up for in enthusiasm. He encouraged the same curiosity in his students that others had tried to stifle in him. That included letting them ask questions during class, which was a big no-no back then.

Albert spent only a couple of years in Zurich before becoming a full professor at the University of Prague. His paycheck was twice

The Miracle Year

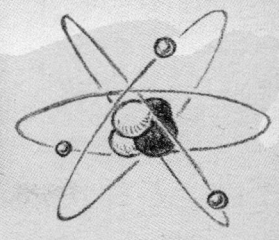

In the same year that Albert published his paper on the special theory of relativity, he also published three others that changed science forever! That's why people later called it his miracle year. Here's a snapshot of the three other papers.

- **PAPER 1: THE PHOTOELECTRIC EFFECT**
  Explains what light is made of and how it moves around.

- **PAPER 2: THE TRUE SIZES OF ATOMS**
  Proves that atoms and molecules exist.

- **PAPER 3: MASS AND ENERGY ($E = mc^2$)**
  E is energy (heat, light, or sound), m is mass (the amount of matter or stuff that makes up something), and c is the speed of light (186,000 miles per second).

as big, which was good since he now had twice the number of kids. His second son, Eduard, was born in 1910. With a new salary and a new home, the Einstein family got to enjoy such comforts as electric lights.

In his new job, Albert's colleagues were many of his science heroes. Not only his work life but also his social life revolved around a set of the biggest and most important thinkers at the time. Life was good for Albert, except for one fact. He and Mileva weren't getting along at all.

The Einsteins moved back to the city where they had once been so happy because the Polytechnic had finally offered Albert a position. But they were far from happy now. By this point nothing could repair Albert and Mileva's marriage, not even returning to Zurich where they had fallen in love. Mileva was often ill and fought with Albert all the time. Albert responded by spending more and more time alone, either traveling or working in his room.

In 1914 Albert changed jobs again! The University of Berlin offered him a position where the only requirement was for him to think and work on his ideas. Although he

wasn't a big fan of Germany, Albert couldn't pass this up.

Mileva tried moving to Berlin, but their relationship in the German city was even worse. She quickly returned to Switzerland with their two sons, Hans Albert and Eduard, and eventually she and Albert divorced.

While in Berlin, Albert fell in love with Elsa Löwenthal. She was actually Albert's first

cousin. He had struck up a friendship with the divorced mother of two and it grew into a relationship.

Nevertheless, Albert was still sad about losing his family and he threw himself entirely into working on his biggest scientific project yet: the general theory of relativity.

CHAPTER FOUR

Space Bender

Albert spent his life looking for unifying principles in physics, meaning ideas that could explain not just a specific phenomenon but many different ones. He believed deeply in an order to the universe and would later in his life look for *the* unifying principle to explain all of physics.

His desire to tie things together drove him to what he called, "the happiest thought of my life," which led to the general theory of relativity.

This idea, explaining gravity, built upon his original special theory of relativity. Newton had given a partial explanation for gravity and how the planets move with his universal law of gravitation—it basically said that the bigger the objects are and the closer they are to each other, the greater their force of attraction. But it didn't explain *why* objects cause gravity.

Enter Albert, who reimagined space and time as coming together as space-time, or a fabric that bends and curves. Gravity is not a force but the result of the bending of space-time when mass is present.

Albert's general theory of relativity explained how Earth (a very, very big bowling ball) warps space so that any object (from a marble out of your hand to light from stars) falls toward it. He didn't just figure out that space bends, but he also found a way to measure how much it bends.

Picture This

In order to understand this idea of how mass causes gravity in space, Gary F. Moring offers this great "thought experiment" in his book *The Complete Idiot's Guide to Understanding Einstein*: Imagine you fill a big swimming pool with clear Jell-O. You take a marble and roll it across the top of the Jell-O. It travels across the surface in a straight line. Now you take a bowling ball and put it in the middle of the swimming pool, which causes a depression in the surface. When you roll your marble

toward the bowling ball, instead of it traveling straight across the surface like it did before, it will roll toward the ball and start circling it. It will continue to circle the bowling ball, as if it were in a funnel. If the Jell-O were completely invisible like space is, you wouldn't see the dent or slope made by the bowling ball and you would think that a hidden force (remember Albert's compass?) was attracting the marble to the bowling ball.

Unlike his special theory of relativity, which took him only weeks to figure out, Einstein's general theory took him nine years, after he began working on it in 1907, to complete. He spent years doing extremely difficult mathematical formulas (and running into problems that meant more math) before coming

up with the long equations that explained his theory. But in 1916 he published the theory that he described as one of "incomparable beauty."

In order to prove the theory was right, astronomers came up with an experiment. They took a star that they knew the exact location of and photographed it right before the star passed behind the sun. If Albert was right, the star would appear higher than its real location as the sun's gravity bent the light coming off it. To get a photo of the star during the day, they had to wait until a solar eclipse, when the moon blocks all the sun's light.

Albert had come out with the general theory of relativity smack in the middle of World War I, which began in 1914. Albert was a **pacifist**, which means he disagreed with wars and didn't believe they came to any good. This put him at odds with some of his German colleagues and he was attacked at the university for his position. Albert firmly believed that scientists should use their powers to help people, not to invent weapons to kill them.

The war also meant the astronomers who hoped to test the general theory of relativity were delayed until the solar eclipse on May 29, 1919. When they finally took the photos, however, the star was in the wrong place. Albert was right!

The news of his discovery made headlines

all over the world. Even if most people couldn't really understand general relativity, they knew it was extremely important. As an article from *The Times* of London read, "Revolution in Science—New Theory of the Universe—Newton's Ideas Overthrown—Momentus Pronoucement—Space 'Warped.'" Almost immediately, Einstein became a world-renowned physicist, the successor to Isaac Newton. That *is* big news.

Albert became an overnight sensation—a bigger star than the one that had proved his theory right. Albert wasn't just famous to scientists. With all the makings of a celebrity (kooky outfits, crazy hair, eccentric personality, great one-liners), he became a huge personality all over the world. Most people didn't know the first thing about relativity, but they knew they liked him. Albert, however, wasn't sure how he felt about fame. This was a guy who said he wanted to be left alone to think.

Elsa, whom he married in 1919, helped Albert manage this strange new aspect of his life. Unlike Mileva, she didn't have a clue about science and didn't want to. She gave Albert the right combination of care and space and good meals.

Once he got used to it, Albert liked giving interviews and soon became a master at them. The short, witty phrases that he became famous for have lived on just like his scientific advancements. Even though journalists, too, had no idea what his science was about, they all wanted to put him in their magazines or papers. His short pants, unbrushed hair, and snappy sound bites turned him into the kind of colorful character the media loves to cover.

Albert Einstein became a household name. Mothers named their children after him, and one tobacco company named a cigar after him. Sacks of letters from fans arrived at his home. He always tried to answer the ones from children even though he was busy solving the mysteries of the universe. One fifteen-year-old girl wrote to him because she needed help with her math homework, and he wrote back! He didn't give her the answer but drew a diagram with a hint so that she could figure it out herself. She eventually did solve the problem, and passed her math class, with Albert's help.

Albert Sounds Off

HERE ARE JUST A FEW OF HIS FAMOUS ONE-LINERS.

"Only a life lived for others is a life worthwhile."

"My life is a simple thing that would interest no one."

"I never worry about the future. It comes soon enough."

"The important thing is not to stop questioning."

"Anyone who has never made a mistake has never tried anything new."

"Why is it that nobody understands me, yet everybody likes me?"

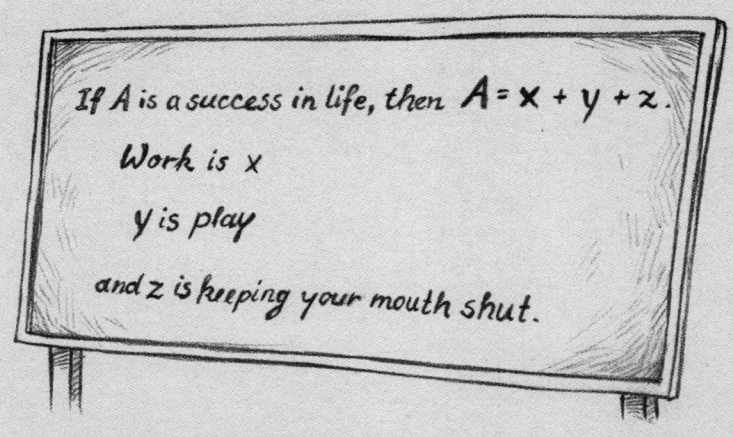

If A is a success in life, then $A = x + y + z$.

Work is x

y is play

and z is keeping your mouth shut.

CHAPTER FIVE

Putting All the Pieces Together

When Albert and Elsa visited the United States for the first time in 1921 after he won the Nobel Prize, thousands of people showed up in New York to greet their boat and the world-famous scientist. Albert was as popular as the biggest movie stars and political leaders of the day. There were parades in his honor, and he was even invited to the White House, where he met President Warren Harding (when he returned to the United States in 1931, Albert met famous

people like Helen Keller). He and Elsa didn't stop at America. They traveled all over the world to the same kind of acclaim.

The one place where Albert wasn't exactly popular was back at home. World War I had left Germany crippled by a huge death toll, a terrible economy, and a scarcity of food. Lots of people, unemployed and unhappy, wanted to find a clear reason for their problems. The Jewish people became this scapegoat. They began to blame the Jews for all their troubles.

Despite Albert's fame and genius, he was not safe from the rise in anti-Semitism; German scientists began to criticize his work simply because he had been born a Jew. Albert hadn't grown up in a religious family or even thought of himself primarily as a Jew (he saw himself as first a human being, then as a scientist), but he didn't try to run away from his identity. These kinds of attacks only strengthened his bond to the Jewish people. As he said himself, "The pursuit of knowledge for its own sake, an almost fanatical love of justice, and the desire for personal independence—these are the features of the Jewish tradition which make me thank my stars that I belong to it."

Albert joined the Zionist movement, whose mission was to create a homeland for the Jews. The purpose of his first trip to the United States was to raise money for a Jewish state. The work of Albert and others just like him resulted in the creation of the state of Israel in 1948.

However, back in 1932, Albert's future was uncertain. Adolf Hitler and his Nazi Party were rising in power with their idea that ridding Germany of all its Jews would solve their problems. Albert in particular was

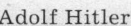
Adolf Hitler

seriously hated by the Nazis. Not only was he a Jew, but he was the most famous Jew in the world. They attacked him and his ideas by burning books he had written and making threats against his life. Still, it took a while to convince Albert to leave his home in Berlin. Like so many others, he couldn't fathom that

six million Jews would be killed in the Nazis' evil plan.

Finally, in December 1932, Albert and Elsa left Germany. It wasn't a moment too soon. About a month later, Hitler and the Nazis (who raided Albert's home) took control of the government. The attack on Jews was immediate and deadly.

The Einsteins settled in America, where Albert took a position at the Institute for Advanced Study in Princeton, New Jersey. He loved America's core value of freedom and settled into a quiet life of work, playing his violin, and spending time with his family. In the suburban New Jersey town, he was an ordinary neighbor, waving to folks on the two-

mile walk he took every day to the Institute and helping kids with their math homework. Elsa passed away in December 1936, leaving Albert with a lot of quiet time.

The quiet didn't last long. World War II broke out in 1939. The United States entered the war on December 7, 1941, after the Japanese, who were on the side of Germany and Italy, bombed Pearl Harbor, a naval base in Hawaii, killing 2,400 people.

Albert was, of course, opposed to war on principle. But World War II presented a more complicated situation. Hitler and the Nazis were terrible and needed to be stopped. To make matters worse, Albert got information that German scientists were working on creating an atomic bomb!

During World War II, Albert heard that the Germans were well on their way to making an atom bomb. Albert found himself in a

Bomb Basics

Albert's revolutionary equation $E = mc^2$ showed that a tiny amount of matter, such as an atom, held a huge amount of energy. This led to the process of nuclear fission (although Albert didn't come up with it). Fission is a process in which the nucleus of an unstable atom splits into two parts, releasing energy and neutrons. This was the basis of the atom bomb, where an unstable atom like uranium is bombarded with particles to split the atom and release the energy inside. One atom splitting only releases a relatively small amount of energy. But as part of a chain reaction with one split atom causing another to split, and on and on, the amount of energy released is enough to destroy a whole city and many of its inhabitants in minutes.

tough situation. He was a pacifist through and through, but if the Nazis controlled such a powerful weapon, they would surely win the war. And that would be terrible for all of humankind.

Devastated that scientists were using his beloved equation $E=mc^2$ for the purposes of war, Albert made a difficult decision and urged President Franklin D. Roosevelt to make an atom bomb first. "Certain aspects of the situation seem to call for watchfulness and, if necessary, quick action on the part of the administration," he wrote in his famous letter from August 2, 1939.

President Roosevelt listened to Albert, and the United States began the top secret Manhattan Project—a project involving a group

of scientists who created an atom bomb in Los Alamos, New Mexico. Even though Albert had made the recommendation, he, like most Americans, had no idea about the Manhattan Project. Because of his very public antiwar views, the government leaders didn't feel they could completely trust Albert to keep the secret.

The secret was revealed after the United States dropped atomic bombs on the Japanese cities of Hiroshima and Nagasaki in August 1945. More than one hundred thousand people were killed. The Japanese surrendered, and World War II ended. Many felt that the atom bomb was a necessary evil to stop a war that was devastating the entire world. But for Albert, the cost of all those civilian deaths was too high.

The aging scientist regretted writing that letter to the president for the rest of his life.

Mahatma Gandhi

Albert spent his later years using his celebrity status to pursue peace. His heroes became people who used nonviolent methods, for change, such as Mahatma Gandhi and African American civil rights leaders. He worked tirelessly to put an end to the use of nuclear weapons. He became an advocate of a world government, so that all countries would work together instead of fighting one another. Unfortunately, most people dismissed Albert as an idealist who dreamed of the impossible, not unlike many scientists had when he published his first important theories.

In addition to peace, Albert continued working on his last big idea: a Theory of Everything. His obsession with what he called the unified field theory, something that would bring together the whole of physics in one idea, began in 1925. Because he didn't like the concept that things happen randomly, he started looking for a single theory that joined together many separate theories on how the universe works. This idea would explain everything from the particles of an atom to the rotation of the planets. His search for this amazing theory led him to a lot of interesting ideas. One of them was the belief that the universe grows and shrinks, and isn't a fixed size as scientists then assumed. In 1929, Edwin Hubble, an astronomer, showed that the universe was expanding. Galaxies are moving farther away from one another, proving Albert right yet again.

He spent the next thirty years searching.

Edwin Hubble

Even after he officially retired, he spent many hours getting tangled up in advanced math, following equations to dead ends, and imagining countless theories; however, he never found that mysterious unifying theory, keeping at it until he died on April 18, 1955. Although he was seventy-six years old, he never lost the same inquisitiveness that he had when just a little boy. "I have no special talents," Albert said. "I am only passionately curious."

10 Things
You Should Know About Einstein

1 Albert Einstein was born to a Jewish family in the small town of Ulm, Germany, on March 14, 1879.

2 He had a big head as a baby and didn't utter a word until he was about two years old, which worried his family that something was wrong with him.

3. His parents, Pauline and Hermann, encouraged their kids to pursue knowledge by asking as many questions as they could come up with.

4. Albert didn't like school when he was a kid because he didn't get along with the other boys, and his teachers thought he was rude for asking too many questions.

5. Albert graduated college from the Swiss Federal Polytechnic Institute in Zurich, and he became a Swiss citizen in 1901.

Swiss flag

6 He worked at the Swiss patent office for eight years, during which he wrote papers on four of his most important theories in one year.

7 Albert was married twice: first to Mileva Maric, with whom he had two sons before their divorce, and then to Elsa Löwenthal, who remained his wife until her death in 1936.

8 When Albert's general theory of relativity was proved correct in 1919, he became an overnight sensation and worldwide celebrity for changing how people think about the universe.

U.S. postage stamp

9 Albert and Elsa fled the Nazis and their German homeland in 1932 and immigrated to America, where he worked hard to make the Zionist dream of a Jewish state a reality.

10 Long after he had retired from the Institute for Advanced Study in Princeton, Albert continued to search for the solution to his last big idea—the unified field theory, an idea that would explain all of physics—but he never found it.

10 MORE Things
That Are Pretty Cool to Know

1 *Einstein Syndrome* is a term that was coined to describe exceptionally bright children who don't talk until much later than the average child.

2 Albert invented a type of refrigerator with another scientist in 1926.

1926 refrigerator

3. Albert kept the notes for his four famous papers in Hans's baby carriage and would take them out while he took the baby on walks outside.

4. Albert worked so hard on his general theory of relativity that he lost a total of fifty pounds!

5. Albert played violin his whole life and his favorite composers were Bach, Schubert, and Mozart. (Another of his favorite hobbies was sailing, even though he couldn't swim.)

6 He never wore pajamas. "I sleep as nature made me," he said.

7 He sold a handwritten copy of his 1905 paper on special relativity for $6.5 million in 1944 and donated the money to the Allied war effort.

8 After Albert's theory of relativity was proved right by the pictures of stars taken during a solar eclipse, he celebrated by buying himself a new violin.

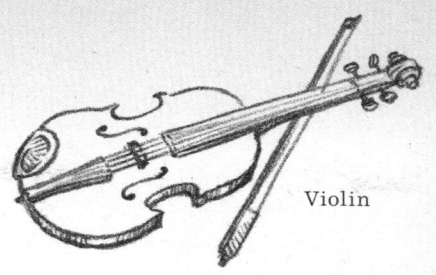
Violin

9 For twenty-two years, FBI agents tapped Albert's phone and went through his mail looking for proof that he was a spy for the Soviet Union.

10 The doctor who performed the autopsy on Albert's body to figure out how he died stole the scientist's brain and kept it for more than forty years.

Places to Visit

Are you interested in experiencing more of Albert's genius? Whether you visit online or in real life, check out these places that contain a piece of his history (or in one case—a piece of his brain!).

Einstein Museum, Princeton, New Jersey
An unofficial museum in the back of a clothing store that houses memorabilia, photographs, and documents from the scientist's life.
landauprinceton.com/einstein-museum

Albert Einstein House, Princeton, New Jersey
nps.gov/nr/feature/JewishHeritage/2007/einstein.htm

The Einstein Memorial, Washington, D.C.
nas.nasonline.org/site/PageServer?pagename=Discover_Collection_Einstein_Memorial_with_slideshow

Mütter Museum, Philadelphia, Pennsylvania
The museum of the College of Physicians of Philadelphia has on display forty-six microscope slides that each contain slices from Albert's brain.
collphyphil.org/site/mutter_museum.html

Einstein House, Bern, Switzerland
einstein-bern.ch/index.php?lang=en

Bibliography

Albert Einstein, Kathleen Krull, Viking, 2009.

Albert Einstein and the Theory of Relativity, Robert Cwiklik, Barron's Educational Series, Inc., 1987.

Albert Einstein: The Giant of 20th Century Science, Judy L. Hasday, Enslow Publishers, 2004.

Albert Einstein: Universal Genius, Mike Venezia, Scholastic, 2009.

Ask Albert Einstein, Lynne Barasch, Farrar, Straus and Giroux, 2005.

The Complete Idiot's Guide to Understanding Einstein, Gary F. Moring, Penguin, 2004.

Did It Take Creativity to Find Relativity, Albert Einstein?, Melvin and Gilda Berger, Scholastic, 2007.

Odd Boy Out: Young Albert Einstein, Don Brown, Houghton Mifflin, 2004.

Glossary

Algebra: a type of mathematics in which symbols and letters are used to represent numbers

Chemistry: the scientific study of substances, what they are composed of, and how they react with each other

Geology: the study of the earth's physical structure, especially its layers of soil and rock

Geometry: the branch of mathematics that deals with points, lines, angles, shapes, and solids

Pacifist: a person who believes very strongly that war and violence are wrong

Patent: a legal document giving the inventor of an item the sole rights to manufacture or sell it

Physics: the science that deals with matter and energy. It includes the study of light, heat, sound, electricity, motion, and force

Prodigy: a person, especially a young one, who has exceptional ability in a particular area, as in *a chess prodigy*

Renaissance: the revival of art and learning, inspired by the ancient Greeks and Romans, that took place in Europe between the 14th and 16th centuries

Index

A
algebra, 27, 108
anti-Semitism, 20–21, 79–80
atomic bomb, 84–88
atoms, 57, 85

B
Berlin, 60, 81

C
chemistry, 29, 108
compass, 8, 11, 18–19
Complete Idiot's Guide to Understanding Einstein, 65–66
Critique of Pure Reason, 29

E
Edison, Thomas, 17
Einstein, Albert, 8, 10–11
   birth, 17, 96
   childhood and education, 4, 6, 12–29, 31–43, 96–97
   death, 93, 103
   divorce, 60, 98
   equations, 4, 5, 57, 85, 86
   fame, 4, 70, 72–73, 77–79, 98
   in family business, 34–35
   immigration to United States, 83–84, 99
   inventions, 100
   letter to President Roosevelt, 86–87, 88
   love of music, 8, 16–18, 101, 102
   marriage, first, 49–50, 59, 98
   marriage, second, 71, 72, 98
   patent office job, 47–49
   peace, pursuit of, 90
   as professor, 56, 58–59
   quotes, 74–75
   science projects, 48–49
   struggle to find job, 43–45
   theories developed by, 50–56
   visits to United States, 77–79, 80

Einstein, Eduard, 9, 11, 58, 60
Einstein, Hans Albert, 9, 11, 49–50, 60, 101
Einstein, Hermann, 8,
   bankruptcy, 45
   business, 16, 31, 34
   compass given to Albert by, 11, 18–19
   curiosity encouraged by, 97
   worries about Albert, 13–14, 32
Einstein, Jakob, 9, 14, 23–25
Einstein, Maja, 6, 9, 10, 14–15
Einstein, Pauline, 8, 13–14, 16–17, 19, 32, 97
Einstein Syndrome, 100
electricity, 40
electric lights, 17, 31, 58
electromagnetic theory, 50
electromagnetism, 40
energy, 57
Europe, map of, 94–95

F
fission, 85
Franklin, Benjamin, 40

G
Galileo Galilei, 38
Gandhi, Mahatma, 90
geology, 29, 108
geometry, 26–27, 108
gravity, 64, 65–66
Greeks, 38
Grossmann, Marcel, 9, 10, 37, 41, 47

H
Harding, Warren, 77
Hiroshima, bombing of, 88
Hitler, Adolf, 80, 84

Hubble, Edwin, 91
Hubble Space Telescope, 92

I
imagination, 7
Institute for Advanced Study, 83, 99
inventions, 4, 7
Israel, 80

J
Jews, 20–21, 79–82

K
Kant, Immanuel, 29
Keller, Helen, 79
knowledge, 7

L
lab explosion, 6, 35, 36
laws of motion, 39, 50
laws of physics, 54
light, 37
   speed of, 57
   traveling on beam of, 6, 29
Löwenthal, Elsa, 9
   background, 60–61
   death, 11, 84
   departure from Germany, 82
   immigration to United States, 11, 99
   marriage, 10, 71, 72, 98
   visit to United States, 77

M
Manhattan Project, 87–88
Maric, Mileva
   divorce, 9, 10, 60, 98
   marriage, 9, 11, 45, 49–50, 59, 98

science background, 41–43, 72
mass, 6, 57, 65–66
Milan, Italy, 11, 31
Moring, Gary F., 65–66

N
Nagasaki, bombing of, 88
nature, laws of, 39
Nazi Party, 80–81
Nazis, 82, 84, 86, 99
Newton, Isaac, 39, 50–51, 54, 70
Nobel Prize in physics, 10, 77
nuclear fission, 85

P
pacifism, 69, 86, 109
patents, 16, 109
Pearl Harbor, 84
photoelectric effect, 10, 57
physics, 6, 29, 35, 37, 38–40, 54, 109
Princeton, New Jersey, 83

R
Renaissance, 38, 109
Roosevelt, Franklin D., 86–87

S
school in Germany, 21–22
Swiss Federal Polytechnic Institute, 10, 35, 97
Swiss patent office, 10, 47–48, 98

T
Talmud, Max, 9, 25–27
Theory of Everything, 90
theory of relativity, general, 10, 61, 63–70, 98, 101, 102

theory of relativity, special, 51–55, 57

U
unified field theory, 90–91, 92, 99
universal law of gravity, 39
universe, 6, 7, 11, 19, 91
University of Berlin, 59–60
University of Prague, 56
University of Zurich, 56

W
World War I, 10, 69, 79
World War II, 11, 84, 88

Z
Zionist movement, 80